12/07

SIMPLE LIFE FORMS

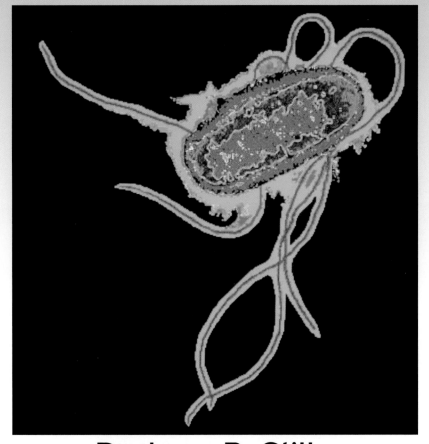

Darlene R. Stille
Contributing author: Carol Ryback

Consultant: Suzy Gazlay, M.A.,
science curriculum resource teacher

Please visit our web site at: www.garethstevens.com
For a free color catalog describing Gareth Stevens Publishing's list
of high-quality books, call 1-800-542-2595 (USA)
or 1-800-387-3178 (Canada).

Library of Congress Cataloging-in-Publication Data available upon request from publisher.

ISBN-13: 978-0-8368-8443-2 — ISBN-10: 0-8368-8443-4 (lib. bdg.)
ISBN-13: 978-0-8368-8452-4 — ISBN-10: 0-8368-8452-3 (softcover)

This edition first published in 2008 by
Gareth Stevens Publishing
A Weekly Reader® Company
1 Reader's Digest Road
Pleasantville, NY 10570-7000 USA

Copyright © 2008 by Gareth Stevens, Inc.

Q2a Media editor: Honor Head
Q2a Media design, illustrations and image search: Q2a Media
Q2a Media cover design: Q2a Media

Gareth Stevens editor: Carol Ryback
Gareth Stevens art direction: Tammy West
Gareth Stevens graphic designer: Dave Kowalski
Gareth Stevens production: Jessica Yanke
Gareth Stevens science curriculum consultant: Suzy Gazlay, M.A.

Photo credits: t=top, b=bottom, m=middle, l=left, r=right
Photolibrary: / SPL / Dr. Linda Stannard, UCT half title, 9; / 15, 41; / John Radcliffe Hospital 17;
/ Sinclair Stammers 25; Andrew Syred 27; / Hybrid Medical Animation 31. Damian Herde: 5.
Shutterstock: / 7. Andrew Syred: 7(t). Nancy Hixson: 7(b). Science Photolibary: / Rickman Godlee:
8(b). CORBIS: / Visuals Unlimited 12. Photolibrary: / Phototake Inc. / Dennis Kunkel 16.
Photolibrary: / Madeleine Openshaw 19. Photo by Don Hamerman for the Institute for Genomic
Biology, University of Illinois: 20. USGS/Cascades Volcano Observatory: / W.Chadwick 21.
Photolibrary: / Peter Arnold Images Inc / A. Murawski Darlyne 29. Dreamstime.com: / Theosid 32; /
Bmcent1 34. Rainbow / Shutterstock: 37(t). Benjamin Fenske: 37(m). Erika Barnes: 37(b). Dennis
Sabo: 38. Photolibrary: / Photo Researchers, Inc. / Mcdaniel Neil 40(t); / Science Source 42.
Konovalikov Andrey: 40(m). Photolibrary: / Pacific Stock / Fleetham Dave 40(bl). Sandra Leidholdt:
40(br). iStockphoto: / 43.

Every effort has been made to trace the copyright holders for the photos used in this book.
The publisher apologizes, in advance, for any unintentional omissions and would be pleased
to insert the appropriate acknowledgments in any subsequent edition of this publication.

Printed in the United States of America

1 2 3 4 5 6 7 8 9 11 10 09 08 07

Contents

Chapter 1 The Smallest Things Alive 4

Chapter 2 Bacteria 9

Chapter 3 Archaea: Extreme Life Forms 18

Chapter 4 Protists 24

Chapter 5 The Fungi Kingdom 30

Chapter 6 Simple Plants and Animals 36

Glossary 44

For More Information 46

Index 47

The Smallest Things Alive

Simple Life Is Everywhere

Simple life forms have existed on Earth for billions of years. The oldest known fossils are 3.5 billion years old. The fossils are of bacteria-like creatures. Today, tiny, simple life forms are all around us without us even knowing. If you looked at your cell phone or a doorknob under a microscope, you could find thousands of simple life forms.

All around us is a world we cannot usually see. Strange life forms ooze and slither. Many of them live in droplets, puddles, ponds, or larger bodies of water. Some of these beings move at a fast and furious pace. They have tiny "tails" that beat and push them through the liquid around them. Others have whirling wheels that propel their bodies along. Still others just float, glistening like jewels. This is a world of alien-looking organisms that is only visible under a microscope. This is the world of simple life forms.

Single-Celled Organisms

All living things are made of cells. Cells are tiny units of life. They have definite boundaries, called

cell walls or cell membranes. Cells can also have many structures inside of them. Some of the structures control what goes on within the cell. Other structures might help the cell move or eat. The simpler the life form, the fewer cells it contains. The simplest life forms of all have only one cell.

One-celled life forms are simple, but they are not dull. They vary greatly in how they look and what

These single-celled organisms can only be seen clearly through a microscope.

they can do. Some simple life forms act like animals. They can move around and must take in food for energy.

Other simple life forms are more like plants. These life forms make their own food using energy from the Sun. Some examples of single-celled life forms include bacteria and amoebas.

Some simple organsims have many cells. They are multicellular life forms. You have probably seen, used, or eaten some of these simple, multicellular organisms. Sponges are a common, very simple multicellular life form. We often eat part of a simple life form on pizza. Mushrooms grow from simple organisms.

Biologists are scientists who study organisms. When

biologists study an organism, they look for a cell structure called a nucleus. The nucleus is the control center of the cell. A cell with a nucleus is a eukaryote cell. We are most familiar with organisms made of one or more eukaryotic cells.

The simplest of all life forms are made of a cell without a nucleus. Such a cell is called a prokaryotic cell. All prokaryotes are single-celled organisms. Not all single-celled organisms are prokaryotes, however.

Where Simple Life Forms Live

Simple life forms live everywhere. Many live in the soil of your backyard and on the floors of tropical rain forests. Many float on the surface of the ocean. Others live inside larger organisms, including human beings. These invisible, simple life forms are all around you. They live on doorknobs, desks,

 Pronunciation Key:

eukaryote (*you-KAR-ee-oat*)

phytoplankton (*FIGH-toe-PLANK-ten*)

prokaryote (*pro-KAR-ee-oat*)

zooplankton (*ZOE-eh-PLANK-ten*)

chairs, and especially on your TV's remote-control device.

Some simple life forms live where nothing else can. They might live in the near-boiling water of hot springs. Others live under rocks in the freezing cold of Antarctica. Still others live deep in the ocean where sunlight never reaches.

Discovery

Scientists discovered simple life forms after the invention of the microscope. Englishman Robert Hooke and Dutchman Anton van Leeuwenhoek were

Plankton

Green algae floats on water.

The surfaces of lakes and oceans are alive with organisms. These floating masses of life are called plankton. Plankton contains a mix of billions of different organisms. Some organisms are single-celled. Others have many cells. Plant-like life forms are called phytoplankton. They make their own food. Algae are simple life forms that are phytoplankton. Zooplankton are more like animals. They must take in food. Phytoplankton and zooplankton mix together as they float.

Plankton is a very important link in the world's food chain. Tiny creatures eat plankton. Larger creatures eat the animals that eat the plankton, and so on. Many larger organisms, such as birds, fish, and whales, can also eat plankton directly.

Simple Life Forms and Infections

Joseph Jackson Lister (1786–1869) improved microsope lenses.

In the 1800s, Joseph Jackson Lister developed an improved microscope. Lister taught his son, Joseph (1827–1912), to use the microscope in his medical practice. Joseph later became a surgeon. In those days, half of all surgery patients died. Dr. Joseph Lister believed that filthy conditions caused infections. He experimented with keeping things clean around his patients. His methods worked. Many of his patients did not get infections.

the first scientists to see this invisible world.

In 1663, Hooke used his microscope to examine bark from a cork tree. Divisions in the bark reminded Hooke of the cells in which prisoners were kept. He named the divisions of cork "cells."

About twenty years later, in 1683, van Leeuwenhoek looked at scrapings from his teeth using a microscope. He saw moving organisms! van Leeuwenhoek called these organisms "animalcules."

What he saw were most likely bacteria. We often call bacteria "germs." These simple life forms can cause many infections and diseases.

A microscopic view of cork reveals individual cells.

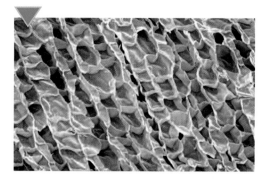

2 Bacteria

All bacteria (the singular form is bacterium) are single-celled organisms. They are the smallest life forms we know about. Bacteria can only be seen with a microscope. There are more bacteria on Earth than any other kind of life form. Imagine a stack of pennies going up from Earth and out into space. If we could make a similar pile using all of the bacteria on Earth, the stack would reach beyond the stars that we can see.

What Bacteria Look Like

Bacteria are prokaryotes. Their cells do not have nuclei. Bacteria have stiff cell walls that give the bacteria their shape. Some bacteria look like rods. Others are round. Still others are curly, like tiny corkscrews. Some

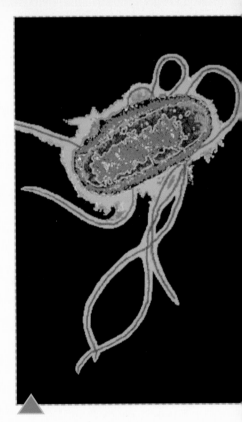

The many "tails," or flagella, of this rod-shaped bacterium help it move.

9

Bugs to drugs

Some bacteriologists are researchers who specialize in studying bacteria. They like to refer to bacteria as "bugs." Many "bugs" are used to develop drugs. Medicines that fight living organisms are called antibiotics. Antibiotics fight infections. The common, germ-killing antibiotic drug called streptomycin is made from *Streptomyces* bacteria. These bacteria grow in long, thin strands called filaments.

bacteria even stick to one another and form long chains.

Some bacteria have extra outside "armor" called a capsule. The capsule protects the bacterium from attack by other organisms. Some bacteria do not have either capsules or cell walls. These bacteria live inside the cells of other organisms.

A structure called a plasma membrane lines the cell wall of a bacterium. The plasma membrane is a like a plastic bag. It holds the cytoplasm in place. Cytoplasm is a gel-like substance that forms the main body of a cell. All the life processes of the bacterium occur within its cytoplasm.

Bacteria also have what look like hairs on their surface. The "hairs" are extensions of the plasma membrane. They stick out through the cell wall. These "hairs" can be different lengths. Long, thin extensions are called flagella. A bacterium can have just one flagellum or many flagella. Bacteria whip or spin their flagella to move themselves along. Other types of bacteria have shorter "hairs" called cilia. A bacterium can be completely covered by cilia. Bacteria use their cilia to move around or to stick to things.

Not all bacteria can move around. Some stay in one spot. Others produce a slimy substance that helps them slither over surfaces.

Where and How Bacteria Live

Bacteria live everywhere, from warm, tropical places to places that are windy and cold. They live in soil, and in the water of lakes, rivers, and oceans. Bacteria thrive indoors on bathroom sinks and kitchen counters. They also live in and on animals and plants.

Like all living things, bacteria need food for energy. They get food in many ways. Some bacteria can make their own food, just as plants do. Blue-green algae are bacteria. Algae make food by using carbon dioxide gas and the energy in sunlight. This process is called photosynthesis. Many kinds of bacteria feed on dead organisms. Other bacteria feed on nonliving substances, such as oil. Some bacteria feed on chemicals, such as sulfur.

Bacteria do not have mouths or internal organs. Food enters a bacterium through its plasma membrane. Wastes also exit through this membrane. The

Oil-Eating Bacteria

Oil tankers carry petroleum across the oceans. If a tanker hits something, oil spills out and pollutes the water and shoreline. It can harm birds, seals, and other sea creatures. Hundreds of such accidents, large and small, occur every year.

The black, gooey oil coats everything it touches. Oil-eating bacteria make special proteins. These proteins break apart the petroleum into chemicals. The bacteria feast on the chemicals and multiply. When all the oil is gone, the bacteria die off. They have nothing left to eat.

membrane only lets certain molecules go into and out of the bacterium. We say the membrane is semipermeable. A semipermeable membrane allows only molecules of a certain size to pass through.

How Bacteria Reproduce

The number of bacteria can double in just a few minutes. One bacterium becomes two, two become four, four become eight, and so on. They can produce millions of copies of themselves within hours.

Like all living things, bacteria have genes made of deoxyribonucleic acid (DNA). In some bacteria, the DNA bunches together in one part of the cell. The DNA of a bacterium can also form an organized structure. In those bacteria, the DNA forms a round structure called a plasmid.

Bacteria cannot be male or female. Instead, they reproduce asexually—usually

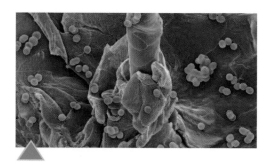

A few bacteria around a hair root and on skin can multiply into millions within hours.

by dividing in two. This kind of reproduction is called binary fission. Well-fed bacteria multiply quickly. First, a bacterium reaches a certain size. Next, its DNA is copied. The copies of DNA move to opposite sides of the bacterium. A new cell wall grows. It divides the original bacterium in half. The two new bacteria are identical to the original. They can each divide to form two more bacteria.

Some bacteria reproduce by growing a small bump, or bud. A copy of the DNA for that bacterium moves into the bud. The bud grows larger and pinches off. It becomes a new bacterium.

🔑 Pronunciation Key:

cytoplasm (*SIGH-toe-plaz-em*)

flagella (*fla-JELL-ah*)

mutation (*mew-TAY-shun*)

photosynthesis
(*FOE-toe-SIN-thuh-sis*)

pneumonia (*new-MO-nya*)

Bacteria can also reproduce a third way. They form spores, which are somewhat like seeds. A spore encloses the bacterium's DNA in a tough covering. Spores are a sort of "resting" state for bacteria. They can survive in this form for millions of years. When conditions are right, the spore will grow into a bacterium.

Bacteria exchange genes in a process called conjugation.

Plasmid in donor bacterium   Recipient bacterium

A conjugation tube, called a sex pilus, forms between donor and recipient bacteria.

Plasmid DNA replication starts. Part of the DNA strand starts moving through the tube.

The recipient bacterium starts copying the transferred DNA.

The DNA in each bacterium forms a plasmid. The bacteria separate.

Most of the time, bacteria reproduce asexually (without transferring DNA). Bacteria can also transfer genes between each other. The transfer process is called conjugation. During conjugation, two bacteria line up. One bacterium extends a long, tail-like structure, called a sex pilus, to the other. Copies of part of the DNA of the first bacterium move along the pilus to the second bacterium. In this way, bacteria can exchange genes.

Helpful Bacteria

Bacteria play a major role in all the environments of the world. Many bacteria are helpful. In the ocean, bacteria that live in plankton help form the base of the world's food chain.

On land, soil could not form without bacteria. Some kinds of bacteria can break down rock. The bacteria produce a strong acid that dissolves minerals out of rock.

Conjugation and Resistance

For many years, drugs called antibiotics killed bacteria. In some cases, antibiotics can no longer kill bacteria. We say these bacteria have developed a resistance to the antibiotics. This happens because the DNA of bacteria changes over time. DNA changes, or mutations, occur during conjugation. The mutations allow the bacteria to multiply in spite of the antibiotics. The new bacteria are resistant to the antibiotics. When resistant bacteria conjugate, they pass on their resistant genes.

The weathering effects of wind, water, and temperature changes also help break rock into smaller and smaller pieces. These rock pieces mix with bits of dead plant and animal matter to form soil. Bacteria help decompose, or break down, this once-living material.

Bacteria that feed on the decaying material help form humus, a valuable part of soil. Humus is rich in nutrients. Plant roots absorb (soak up) nutrients from the humus in the soil. If not for bacteria that help create humus, the world would overflow with dead material.

We use bacteria for a number of important tasks. In addition to helping clean up oil spills, bacteria "work" in sewage treatment plants. They help break down human waste and make dirty water clean again.

Some bacteria help other living things get the nutrients they need. Nitrogen is a key plant nutrient. Nitrogen is a gas in Earth's atmosphere. But it is not in a form that plants can use. It must be "fixed," or changed, into a form that plants can absorb.

Nitrogen-fixing bacteria perform this task. Some nitrogen-fixing bacteria live independently. Others live on plants. Nitrogen-fixing bacteria form lumps, called nodules, on the roots of legumes, such as peas and beans.

Bacteria also help animals digest food. Bacteria live in the stomachs of cows, sheep, goats, and other grazing animals. These bacteria help the animals digest tough plant parts.

A type of bacterium called *Escherichia coli* ("*E. coli*") lives in human intestines. *E. coli* helps people and other animals digest food. When *E. coli* grows on food, however, it causes serious infections.

Harmful Bacteria

E. coli is only one of many species (kinds) of bacteria that can cause illness. If *E. coli* is

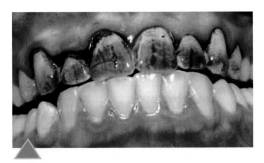

Bacteria feed on plaque, the thin film that forms on teeth. Bacteria produce acids that cause teeth to rot.

found in lakes or streams, it usually means that there is a sewage leak nearby. *E. coli* in food, on your hands, or on eating utensils can cause intestinal distress in humans.

Strep throat is caused by Group A *Streptococcus* bacteria. These are round bacteria that live in the nose and throat. They are spread by coughs and sneezes. The symptoms of this infection include a sore throat, fever, and a throat rash.

Bacteria also cause tooth decay. Mouth bacteria form a sticky film called plaque. Plaque clings to teeth. The plaque bacteria feed on starches and sugars left in your mouth after you eat. As these bacteria grow, they produce an acid that dissolves tooth enamel. Frequent brushing and flossing help remove plaque.

Before the discovery of antibiotics, many people died from bacterial infections. A small cut or scratch that became seriously infected

Sick Bacteria

A bacterium itself can be made "sick" by another organism, called a virus. A virus is much smaller than a bacterium. Once inside another organism, such as a bacterium, a virus can reproduce. It makes many copies of itself. The virus takes over that bacterium. The virus has infected the bacterium.

could cause death. Bacteria can cause other illnesses.

Pneumonia is a serious lung infection caused by bacteria. It was once a leading cause of death in the United States. Antibiotics helped reduce the number of people who died from pneumonia.

Tuberculosis is another serious lung infection. Before antibiotics were in common use, people with tuberculosis spent months or even years in special hospitals. The bacterium that causes tuberculosis has become resistant to many antibiotics. The disease is becoming a serious global problem again.

Simple life forms and food

Some bacteria cause food to spoil. Other bacteria are used to make food. Many foods, such cheese and yogurt, could not be made without bacteria. Yeasts are simple life forms that help break down sugars. This process is called fermentation. Yeasts help bread rise. They also produce alcohol in wine and beer.

Yeasts are simple life forms.

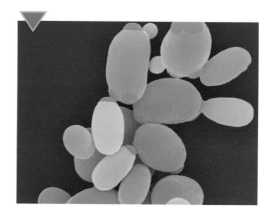

Lyme disease

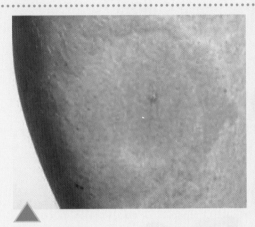

A bull's-eye rash is a sign of Lyme disease.

Ticks are related to spiders. They bite animals and feed on their blood. Ticks can transfer diseases between animals. The tiny black-legged tick (deer tick) can carry a bacterium that causes Lyme disease.

Lyme disease causes flu-like symptoms (signs). The person may have a fever, headache, muscle aches, and fatigue. Someone with Lyme disease may develop a round or oval rash. The rash is red on the edges and pale in the center.

The rash can show up on the arms, legs, back, and other places on the body.

Lyme disease bacteria usually live in mice, other small mammals, and deer. When a tick bites one of these infected animals, it sucks up the bacteria along with blood. The bacteria live in the tick's gut. Ticks cannot fly or jump. They wait on leaves of bushes or grasses. When an animal brushes against the plant, the tick attaches to the animal. Not all ticks carry Lyme disease. But if an infected tick bites a human, that person may soon develop symptoms of Lyme disease.

If left untreated, Lyme disease can lead to major health problems. Lyme disease affects the joints, nervous system, and heart. Antibiotics can kill the bacterium that causes Lyme disease.

3 Archaea: Extreme Life Forms

Tiny Archaeans

Archaeans are usually less than 0.00004 of an inch (1 micron) long. Archaeans look like dots, even if magnified many hundreds of times. Scientists must use a powerful microsope called an electron microscope to view an archaean's physical characteristics.

Biologists once thought that life existed only in certain places and under certain conditions. The places could not be too hot or too cold. They could not be too salty or contain strong chemicals. Some environments simply seemed too harsh to support life.

In the 1960s, biologists began examining the hot springs in Wyoming's Yellowstone National Park. They found microorganisms living there. The biologists dipped microscope slides fastened to poles into the steaming pools.

When the biologists studied those slides under a microscope, they were suprised to find single-celled organisms. The strange organisms did not have a nucleus.

They were prokaryotes. The organisms looked like very weird bacteria—but they weren't bacteria. The biologists had discovered a new kind of life!

Simple life forms and mineral deposits help give hot springs in Yellowstone National Park their colors.

Carl R. Woese discovered archaea.

A New Class of Life

A microbiologist is someone who studies very tiny life forms. Microbiologist Carl R. Woese directed the Yellowstone project. He studied the genes in these new life forms. He also studied the chemicals they produced.

Woese made a startling discovery. The new organisms living in the hot springs produced chemicals unlike those made by any known bacteria. In some ways, these life forms seemed more like animal cells than like bacteria. Woese decided that these strange life forms were not bacteria at all. They represented an entirely different kind of life form. Woese named these new life forms "archaea."

Woese's discovery changed how we classify all forms of life. Since the 1950s, biologists had grouped all living things into five Kingdoms. These Kingdoms were Animalia, Plantae, Fungi, Protista, and Monera. At first, most scientists thought that bacteria and archaeans belonged in the Kingdom Monera.

Woese believed there were three groups even larger than Kingdoms. He identified three Domains—Archaea, Eubacteria (the true bacteria), and Eukaryota. The Archaea and Eubacteria Domains include all the prokaryotes. Eukaryota includes all organisms with cells that have a nucleus.

Where They Live

Archaea seem to live everywhere on Earth. Many archaeans live in normal environments. Other archaeans live in extreme environments where nothing else can live. One group of archaeans thrives in nearly boiling water. Some live at the bottom of the oceans around sulfurous vents. They can also live in soil around volcanoes. Another group

Scientists look for archaea in extreme places, such as the sulfurous soil around volcanoes.

lives in the freezing water and cold, rocky soil of Antarctica.

One group of archaeans produces methane gas as a waste product. Methane is a colorless, odorless gas. These archaeans cannot live in our normal atmosphere. Oxygen would poison them. They must live in oxygen-free environments. Such archaeans use carbon dioxide, hydrogen, and other chemicals to create energy. For instance, they might live in the thick, dense mud of wetlands. Others thrive in

sewage treatment plants. Still more live in the intestines of cows and other animals, and inside termites.

Another type of archaean loves salt. They live in salt flats and very salty bodies of water. They are found in the Dead Sea in the Middle East and in Great Salt Lake in Utah. The cells of other organisms would lose most of their water and die in these salty environments. Salt-loving archaeans somehow balance the salt levels inside and outside their cells.

Other extreme-living archaeans thrive in the toxic waters coming from the Iron Mountain Mine in northern California. Mining metals

there had caused terrible pollution. Water in the mine was like battery acid. It could eat through skin. Scientists searching for extreme life forms wore gloves and thick rubber boots to protect their feet. Nevertheless, some archaeans were living very comfortably there. They had developed an outer coat that acted like armor to protect them from being destroyed by the acid.

One of the strangest environments on Earth is found deep on the ocean floor. Extremely hot water gushes up through holes called hydrothermal (hot water) vents. Melted rock inside Earth heats the water, which contains a lot of suffur. No sunlight reaches these vents because they are so deep. The archaeans and other life forms found around these vents depend on sulfur for energy. Other strange creatures, such as giant tube worms, feed on the archaeans and other life forms.

🔑 Pronunciation Key:

Archaea (*ar-KEY-uh*)
Eubacteria (*YOU-bak-TIR-ee-ah*)
hydrothermal
(*HIGH-droh-THER-mal*)

Did Archaeans Come First?

Many scientists believe that archaeans could have been the first life forms on Earth. Our planet was only about one billion years old when archaeans first appeared. Few plants or animals alive today could have survived Earth's harsh early environment. There was very little oxygen and Earth's atmosphere was mostly made of ammonia. Temperatures everywhere were probably very hot.

Scientists used a clever method to look for signs of the first archaeans. They searched for chemicals that could only have come from decaying archaeans. They found such chemicals in rock that contains oil. They found such rock in several places, including Greenland. In the extreme conditions of Earth 3.8 billion years ago, these archaeans were common life forms.

Archaea on Mars?

Since the space age began in the late 1950s, we have sent space probes to explore our solar system. So far, those probes have not discovered any life forms on other planets.

Scientists once believed that all life forms needed sunlight, oxygen, and water. Now, many scientists hope to determine whether or not extreme life forms similar to archaeans lie buried under the dry soil of Mars. They also program space probes to detect any type of life form that might thrive in the poisonous atmospheres of other planets or on their moons. Still other scientists are researching the possibility that life in the form of archaeans arrived on Earth from another solar system.

4 Protists

Malaria

Malaria is a disease caused by four different protists from the Genus *Plasmodium*. These organisms live inside mosquitoes. If an infected mosquito bites an animal, the animal can get malaria. Each year, malaria kills more than one million people worldwide.

If you look at a drop of swamp water under a microscope, you will probably see what look like tiny animals swimming around. You may also see what look like tiny green plants. These tiny organisms are actually life forms called protists. Protists live in all parts of the world, mainly in the ocean, lakes, rivers, and other bodies of water.

Most protists are single-celled. Protists are different from bacteria and archaeans. All protists are eukaryotes. They have cells with a nucleus. The nucleus contains the genes of the protist. Its cytoplasm contains tiny structures called organelles. The organelles carry out all the processes of life. Protists are not animals, plants, or fungi. They

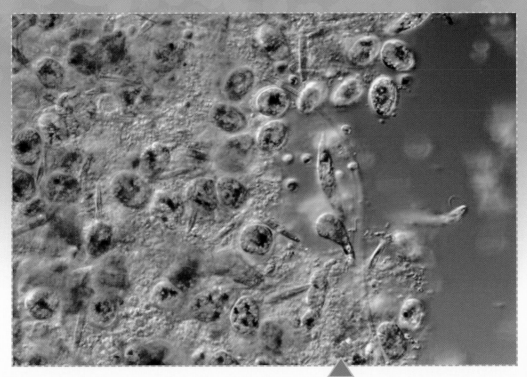

are organisms that do not fit in any other kingdom.

The protist kingdom contains a huge variety of organisms. Some protists live as single cells. Others form groups called colonies or long filaments. A few protists are multicellular (have more than one cell). Some protists make their own food through photosynthesis. Other protists behave more like animals and must find food to eat.

Euglena are protists. They make their own food, like plants. Euglena also display some animal characteristics. They are active swimmers.

Getting Around

Some protists move around while others stay in one place. The protists that move have some

Red Tides and Dinoflagellates

Have you ever heard of a red tide? Red tides occur in ocean waters along the coastlines around the world. Despite the name, the water does not always turn red. It could be brown, orange, or yellow. Most "red tides" are caused by a sudden explosion in the number of protists called dinoflagellates in the area. An increase in the dinoflagellate population can kill other sea creatures. Sometimes, the sea creatures die because the protists that cause the red tide use up all the oxygen in the water. Dinoflagellates can also give off poisons that kill other organisms, such as fish and crustaceans. A red tide can make the water glow at night. Chemicals in the cells of the dinoflagellates produce the glow, called bioluminescence.

interesting ways of getting around.

Under the microscope, amoebas look like water-filled plastic bags that are always changing shape. They move by pushing their cytoplasm out against their cell membrane. This motion changes their shape and creates pseudopods, or false feet. Amoebas live in freshwater and in the bodies of animals. Some amoebas can cause illness in people.

Like bacteria, some protists have flagella or cilia. (Cilia means "eyelash" in Latin.) Protists move by using tail-like flagella or hair-like cilia. Flagellates are protists with flagella. A ciliate is a protist that is covered with cilia. A paramecium is a common ciliate. It moves by beating its cilia.

The Tests of Protists

Some protists produce a rigid "skeleton"—much like a shell—that protects the

A close-up of a foraminiferan test reveals a delicate structure.

in warm water near the equator. Foraminiferans live everywhere in the ocean. They also live on the seafloor and in beach sand. The tests of some foraminiferans can color the sand. Sand on the island of Bermuda is pinkish because of billions of foraminiferan tests.

animal inside. It is made from silica, the main ingredient in sand. The correct name for the "skeleton" is a "test."

Diatoms and radiolarians make their tests from silica. They look like delicate glass ornaments. Other protists make their tests from calcium carbonate (limestone). Foraminiferans use calcium carbonate to make tests. The tests can grow to be about 8 inches (20 centimeters) long.

Many diatoms live in freshwater. They also live in saltwater. Radiolarians are usually found floating among the plankton on the ocean's surface. Most radiolarians live

"Seaweed" and Other Algae

People often call algae that grow in the ocean "seaweed." There are three kinds of algae—green, brown, and red. Most green algae live in freshwater lakes, streams, and ponds. Some species live around rocks on ocean beaches. Anyone who has swum in a lake or walked along an ocean beach has probably seen some type of green algae.

In warm weather, the water in small ponds and roadside ditches is often covered with a green scum. The scum belongs to a species of green algae called *Spirogyra*. It forms long strands called filaments. They tangle together to form a film on the water.

One of the most familiar and spectacular types of algae is the multicellular giant kelp. Kelp is a brown alga. ("Alga" is the singular form of "algae.") It grows in cool water along the coasts of continents. Some of the largest kelp in the world grows along the coast of California.

Giant kelp form underwater forests. Kelp grows on a stalk called a stipe. "Holdfasts" anchor the kelp to the seafloor. Air-filled structures called pneumatocyts act like ballons to keep the kelp leaves ("blades") afloat.

Some giant kelp grow as tall as a ten-story building. Hundreds of sea creatures live in kelp forests.

Slime Molds

Slime molds are protists that look like alien blobs. They live in damp places on land, such as decaying tree stumps.

Some slime molds have cells that join together like one gigantic cell with many nuclei. Other slime molds are made of individual cells that clump together. Slime molds can creep slowly over surfaces. Like amoebas, slime molds move by extending pseudopods.

Protist Food

Some protists have interesting ways of taking in food. An amoeba, for example, surrounds bacteria, algae, or other food particles with its pseudopods. The amoeba then makes a kind of bubble. The bubble contains fluid that digests the food. Green, brown, and red algae make their own food through photosynthesis.

Another group of protists, called Euglena, displays traits common to both plants and animals. When Euglena are in sunlight, they capture energy from the Sun to make food. When they are in darkness, Euglena take in particles of food in much the same way as amoebas. Euglena have an eyespot that senses light and dark. They move by waving a flagellum. Euglena live on the surface of freshwater ponds. Like *Spirogyra*, they form a green surface scum.

How Protists Reproduce

Protists reproduce in a variety of ways. Most reproduce asexually by binary fission. Amoebas and Euglena, for example, simply divide in half. Single-celled algae also reproduce by splitting. Like bacteria, some protists reproduce using conjugation. Paramecia

Diatoms have delicate structures.

exchange genes through conjugation.

Diatoms reproduce either asexually or sexually. Their tests are in two pieces, like a box and lid. The two parts separate easily during binary fission. Diatoms can also produce male and female sex cells. These cells unite to form a new diatom.

Single-celled algae can reproduce by budding. Other algae have a complicated way to form male and female cells and can reproduce sexually.

 Pronunciation Key:

cilia (*SI-lee-ah*)

Euglena (*YOU-glee-nah*)

foraminiferan (*fo-RAH-mi-NI-fer-an*)

organelles (*OR-guh-NELLZ*)

29

5 The Fungi Kingdom

D o you like mushrooms on your pizza? If so, you are eating part of an organism from one of the major Kingdoms—the Fungi Kingdom. Mushrooms are the reproductive organs of certain fungi. (The word "fungus" is singular. The word "fungi" is plural.)

In all, more than fifty thousand different kinds of fungi exist. Other fungi include molds (other than slime molds), mildew, and yeast. All fungi are eukaryotes. They may be unicellular (one-celled) or multicellular.

Some fungi live in water. Some live on moist material on land. Other fungi are parasites. They feed on living organisms, called hosts. Parasites can live on host plants or host animals.

Symbiosis: good and bad

Symbiosis is a fancy way to say that two organisms live together. Sometimes, both benefit from the relationship. Other times, only one does. In other cases, one organism is harmed.

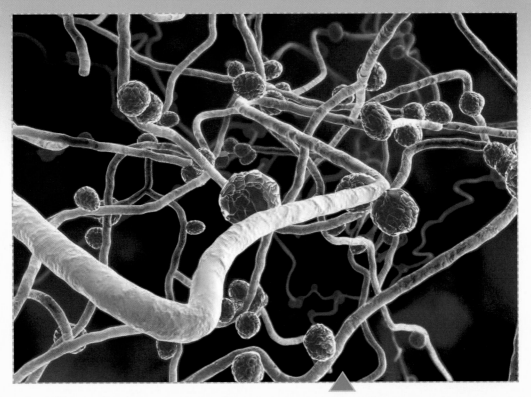

A parasitic relationship harms or even kills the host. Other kinds of fungi live in a sort of partnership with another plant or animal. Neither organism suffers from the relationship. A relationship in which neither organism is harmed is called a mutualistic relationship.

Fungi are simple life forms. They consist of long strands, or filaments,

This fungus has many long filaments, called hyphae. All fungi have hyphae except yeasts.

The World's Largest Life Form

The largest organism on Earth is a honey mushroom. You cannot see most of it. The bulk of its body grows underground. It lives in the Malheur National Forest in the Blue Mountains of eastern Oregon. This mycelium is about 3.5 miles (5.6 kilometers) across. The entire fungus would fill more than 1,600 football fields.

Parts of this honey mushroom appear above the surface.

that grow tightly together. A filament grows by adding cells to the ends. These filaments are called "hyphae." A mass of hyphae strands is called the mycelium. The mycelium is the main body of a fungus. In most cases, the mycelium of a fungus is not visible. It grows underground or is contained within another substance.

How Fungi Get Food

Fungi do not have mouths, stomachs, or any way to digest food. That means fungi do not eat like an animal eats. Fungi also do not make their own food, like plants. Still, fungi need nourishment. They live and grow by another method. Fungi absorb nutrients from matter around them.

Fungi are decomposers. They "feed" by breaking down other materials. Most fungi live on and "eat" dead leaves, rotting wood, and other decaying matter. Their hyphae give off chemicals. These chemicals help decompose the plant or animal matter. The fungi then absorb the decomposed matter. The decaying matter is slowly used up.

As a fungus absorbs the decomposed materials, it grows bigger. It can also send its hyphae deeper into any material that is left. If the decaying matter is all used up, the filaments stretch farther into the soil of the surrounding area. The mycelium keeps growing.

The Life of a Mushroom

Take a walk in a wooded area. You may see mushrooms growing in moist, shady soil under leaves and trees. The most familiar mushroom

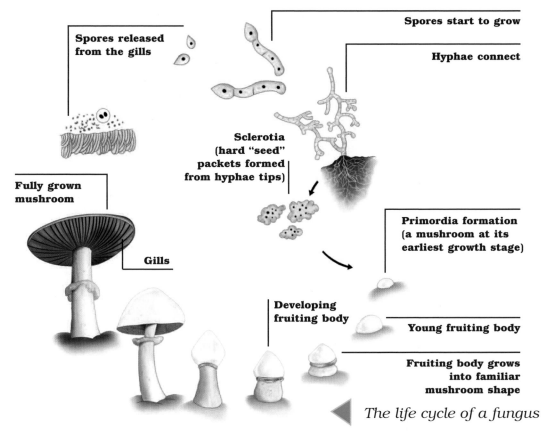

Spores released from the gills

Spores start to grow

Hyphae connect

Sclerotia (hard "seed" packets formed from hyphae tips)

Fully grown mushroom

Primordia formation (a mushroom at its earliest growth stage)

Gills

Developing fruiting body

Young fruiting body

Fruiting body grows into familiar mushroom shape

The life cycle of a fungus

Lichen

Lichen grow all over the world. You might find a lichen growing on bare rock. A lichen consists of a fungus and an alga joined together in a mutualistic relationship. The fungus can join with a protist, such as some type of green algae. It can also join with a bacterium, such as a type of blue-green algae—also called cyanobacteria. The green algae or the cyanobacteria use photosynthesis to produce food for the fungus. The fungus provides a "house" for the algae. The house is a structure made of filaments. It protects the algae from the weather. Any lichen growth is a sign of a healthy environment. Lichen do not grow well in polluted areas.

Lichen often grow on rock.

shape looks like a smooth cap growing on top of a stalk. If you look on the underside of the cap, you may see delicate slits, called gills.

Mushrooms can also have wrinkled caps. "Woody" mushrooms are fungi that look like flat flower petals growing out of tree trunks.

"Mushroom" is not a scientific name of an organism. A mushroom is a reproductive part. It grows from the mycelium. Mushrooms produce spores that produce more fungi.

Spores are one stage in the sexual reproduction of fungi. One spore has only half of the genes needed to produce a new fungus. A fungus begins growing when a male and female spore meet. One spore has a filament that reaches out to the other spore. They join to form one cell with two nuclei. Eventually, that cell grows into filaments that form a mycelium. Mushrooms later pop up from the mycelium. The fungus releases spores from the gills, and the cycle begins again.

Useful Yeast

Yeast are single-celled fungi. They reproduce by budding and through spores. Yeasts grow in soil and saltwater. We use yeasts to ferment sugars. Fermentation gives off carbon dioxide gas. This is the gas that makes bread dough rise. Yeasts are also used for making products that contain alcohol, such as beer and wine.

Yeast may also help reduce air pollution. Corn, sugar cane, and other crops fermented with yeast produce ethanol. Ethanol is a type of alcohol that can be added to gasoline. A gasoline-ethanol mix gives off fewer polluting chemicals than pure gasoline.

Pronunciation Key:

ethanol (EH-tha-nal)
hyphae (*HIGH-fee*)
lichen (*LIE-ken*)
mutualistic (*mew-choo-wi-LIS-tick*)
mycelium (*my-SEE-lee-um*)

Fungi and Plants

Many plants could not live without fungi. The plants and the fungi form a mutualistic relationship. The fungi live in the roots of some plants. The fungi filaments reach far beyond the roots and absorb nutrients for the plant. Through photosynthesis, plants provide food for the fungi.

6 Simple Plants and Animals

Mosses and Pollution

Mosses cannot control the water they gain and lose. Chemicals and pollutants in rain and in the air become concentrated in the mosses' tissues. Scientists sample the mosses to monitor air pollution chemicals and check for changes.

People know that oak trees or roses are plants. They know that a dog or an elephant is an animal. All of the plants and animals that we normally see contain many billions of specialized cells. They are complex organisms. A large number of very simple plants and animals also exist.

Nonvascular Plants

Mosses, liverworts, and hornworts are simple plants. They have no stems or leaves. Simple plants are nonvascular. They do not have an internal tube system for the flow of nutrients. Nonvascular plants grow close to the ground. They absorb (take in) their food and water directly from the moist ground.

Mosses (top), liverworts (middle), and hornworts (bottom) are simple plants.

Simple plants can absorb water by osmosis or capillary action. Osmosis involves the movement of fluids across a membrane or barrier, such as a cell wall. Capillary action relies on the stickiness of water molecules to each other.

Mosses grow tightly together on damp rocks or soil. They form thick mats that look like lush carpets. Liverworts look very similar to mosses. Hornworts look like they have a green horn growing out of the top of the plant.

Sponges

Your rectangular kitchen sponge is not a real sponge. Real sponges are living animals. They have odd shapes and come in many colors. An adult sponge does not move around. Scientists once thought that sponges were plants.

Most sponges live in saltwater. A few live in freshwater. A sponge is made up of millions of cells.

Some of the sponge cells have specialized tasks. The cells do not form any body organs, however. Instead, the inside of a sponge is like a network of tunnels.

Sponges reproduce by budding. They also reproduce sexually. At certain times of the year, sponges eject their sex cells in huge clouds all at once. Male and female cells join to form sponge larvae. The larvae float around until they attach to an underwater object. New sponges grow from the larvae.

Tube sponges often grow in bunches, called colonies.

Animals With Stinging Cells

Jellyfish are not actual fish. They belong to a group of animals called Cnidarians. Other Cnidarians include corals, anemones, and sea wasps.

Jellyfish are simple animals without backbones. Instead of brains, they have a network of nerves. Jellyfish can sense light and dark and other changes in their environment.

Their main body often has a bell shape. The bell of a jellyfish has muscles that tighten and relax to move the creature through the water.

Cubozoans, or box jellyfish, have a "square" bell. Some are harmless. Others are deadly. A cubozoan called the Arctic Lion's Mane is among the most poisonous sea animals known. Its sting has enough poison to kill about fifty humans. Like many jellyfish species, it roams the oceans.

Many Cnidarians have tentacles. Tentacles hang from

Building a Coral Reef

Corals are Cnidarians. They live most of their lives as polyps. Each polyp has tiny tentacles to catch food particles. Coral polyps grow in colonies. Microscopic algae live in the coral. The coral protects the algae. In return, the algae provide the coral with some of its food through photosynthesis. Some corals absorb calcium carbonate from seawater. When the coral polyps die, their skeletons remain to form limestone coral reefs. Another layer of coral polyps settles on top of the reef, and the reef building continues.

the bell. The tentacles of some jellyfish can get as long as 100 feet (30 meters). Tentacles can wrap around prey. The tentacles, and sometimes the bell itself, contain thousands of specialized stinging cells.

39

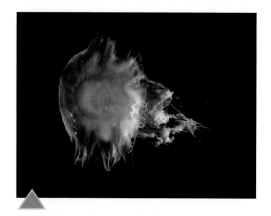

The Arctic Lion's Mane jellyfish sting can be deadly.

The colored portions are these jellyfishes' reproductive organs.

The medusa stage of a jellyfish

The stinging cells, called nematocysts, can shoot out tiny poisonous "harpoons." The nematocysts inject poison into whatever they hit. The poison numbs any prey the Cnidarians catch with their tentacles.

Cnidarians have a two-stage life cycle, the polyp and the medusa. In the polyp stage of a jellyfish's life, the creature attaches itself to an object and does not move. Its free-swimming stage is the medusa stage. The creature moves about as a clear jellyfish. When we think of a jellyfish, we usually picture the medusa stage. When we think of a coral, however, we usually picture the polyp stage.

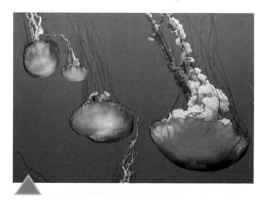

Jellyfish often have long, stinging tentacles.

Flatworms, Roundworms, and Earthworms

Flatworms are Planarians—simple animals that live in shallow water. They have long bodies and a head shaped like a triangle. The head contains eyespots and a mouth. The mouth of a flatworm can suck the insides out of other organisms. Tapeworms are another type of flatworm. They live as parasites in the intestines of other animals. A flatworm is a hermaphrodite. It has both male and female sex organs.

Roundworms are also called Nematodes. Nematodes include hookworms and pinworms. They have long, thin bodies with a long, thin gut. Their bodies are like a tube within a tube. Many Nematodes are parasites. They cause diseases in humans and other animals. Some Nematodes produce up to 27 million eggs at a time! Your puppy or kitten may have once had roundworms, hookworms, or tapeworms.

 Pronunciation Key:

Cnidarian (*nigh-DARE-ee-an*)

cholera (*KOL-le-rah*)

hermaphrodite
(*her-MAH-frow-dyet*)

Cholera

Cholera is a disease caused by a bacterium that infects the small intestine. People get cholera by drinking water or eating food contaminated by the bacteria. Symptoms include bloody diarrhea, intestinal cramps, and vomiting. People with cholera may die from fluid loss and shock.

Vibrio cholerae *causes cholera.*

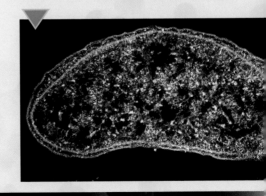

Alexander Fleming and the Discovery of Penicillin

Alexander Fleming at work.

Alexander Fleming was born on a farm in Scotland in 1881. He went to medical school in London, England. Fleming became a doctor in 1906. At that time, biologists had just discovered that bacteria caused infections. Also around that time, surgeons were finally realizing the need to keep wounds clean. Once bacteria got into the body, however, doctors had no treatment to offer their patients.

Bacteria can also cause diseases in otherwise healthy people. For instance, anyone can catch the bacteria that cause pneumonia. Fleming began to look for ways to kill bacteria.

In 1928, Fleming accidentally discovered penicillin. He was growing molds in laboratory dishes. Molds are another simple life form. Some mold got into a laboratory dish in which he was growing bacteria. Fleming noticed that the bacteria touched by the mold died. He experimented with the mold, called *Penicillium notatum*. Fleming realized that something in the mold had killed the bacteria. He named the bacteria-killing substance after the mold. Penicillin eventually became the world's first antibiotic. An antibiotic is a medicine that fights bacteria.

The earthworm is a very useful animal. Like other worms, an earthworm's body is a long tube inside a tube. The outside of an earthworm has sections, called segments. The segments look like rings around the worm's body.

Earthworms burrow into the soil. They make tunnels and loosen the ground. As soil passes through their bodies, any decaying matter in the soil is broken down. Microscopic organisms also in the soil break down the decaying matter even further. The activities of earthworms and simple life forms help plant roots absorb nutrients. Animals and people eat the plants. In this way, all life on Earth has some connection to simple life forms.

Earthworms improve the soil.

Bacteriologists

Bacteriologists are scientists who study helpful and harmful bacteria. Some bacteriologists work in hospitals or medical centers. They look for signs of bacterial infections. Other bacteriologists work in public health laboratories. They examine food and water samples to check for disease-causing bacteria. Many bacteriologists work for drug companies. They study what makes bacteria become resistant to antibiotics. They also help develop new drugs that kill bacteria.

Bacteriology careers require a college degree. Someone who wants to become a bacteriologist takes courses in biology and chemistry. Most bacteriologists earn an advanced degree, such as a master's degree or a Ph.D.

Glossary

amoeba a one-celled protozoan with no set shape that lives in saltwater or freshwater and can cause diseases

antibiotic a drug that fights a bacterial infection

carbon dioxide a gas in air used by plants to make food

cilia tiny, hair-like projections on microscopic organisms

conjugation the method by which bacteria exchange genes

cytoplasm the gel-like main part of a cell

decomposer an organism that breaks down wastes and dead plant or animal matter

DNA (deoxyribonucleic acid) the chemical that contains the code for the development of an organism

eukaryote an organism whose cells have a nucleus

fission the splitting apart of one cell into two cells

flagella hair-like "tails" that help microorganisms move

hermaphrodite an organism with both male and female sex cells or sex organs

hydrothermal relating to warm or hot water

hyphae the "threads" that make up the mycelium of a fungus

mutation a change in a gene

mycelium the filaments or threads called hyphae that make up the largest portion of the underground body of a fungus

nematocyst the stinging cell of sea creatures called Cnidarians

nodule a bacteria-filled lump on a plant root that converts nitrogren gas to a usable form **nonvascular** characterized by the lack of a tube-like, internal vessel system

organelle any of several tiny structures in the cytoplasm that performs a particular job

osmosis the flow of molecules through a semipermeable membrane from an area of low concentration to an area where the concentration is higher

photosynthesis the process by which plants and algae make food using sunlight, carbon dioxide, and water

phytoplankton tiny floating plants that help form plankton

plankton a mass of simple life forms that floats near the ocean surface and provides food for higher life forms, such as whales

plaque a sticky film of bacteria that grows on and coats teeth

plasmid a circular form of DNA found in bacteria

pneumonia a lung disease caused by bacteria or viruses

prokaryote a cell that does not have a nucleus

pseudopod a false foot created by a single-celled organism as it projects its cytoplasm against the cell membrane

tuberculosis a lung disease caused by bacteria

virus a capsule of simple genes inside a protein coat that infects a cell and directs it to make copies of the virus

zooplankton simple animals and one-celled organims that float in the plankton

For More Information

Books

Cerullo, Mary M.
Sea Soup: Phytoplankton.
Tilbury House (1999)

Cerullo, Mary M.
Sea Soup: Zooplankton.
Tilbury House (2001)

King, Katie. *Protists and Fungi.* Discovery Channel School Science: Universes Large and Small (series).
Gareth Stevens (2003)

Latta, Sara L. *The Good, the Bad, the Slimy: The Secret Life of Microbes.* Enslow (2006)

Rhodes, Mary Jo.
Life in a Kelp Forest.
Children's Press (2006)

Souza, Dorothy M.
What Is a Fungus?
Franklin Watts (2002)

Viegas, Jennifer. *Fungi and Molds: Germs! The Library of Disease-Causing Organisms.*
Rosen (2004)

Web sites

www.fi.edu/tfi/units/life/
Check out this Web site for a wealth of information about all living organisms.

www.mbayaq.org/efc/living_species/print.asp?inhab=479
Learn more about giant kelp from the Monterey Bay Aquarium's Web site.

www.microbeworld.org/
Watch a video about microbes or explore the "In the News" or "Meet the Microbes" links for more information.

http://commtechlab.msu.edu/sites/dlc-me/zoo/
Spend a day at a virtual microbial zoo.

www.fsis.usda.gov/OA/food safetymobile/mobilegame.swf
Answer food-safety questions as you take a virtual drive through Food Safety Park.

http://oceanlink.island.net/oinfo/seaweeds/seaweeds.html
Follow the links to discover more about the many kinds of seaweed.

Publisher's note to educators and parents: Our editors have carefully reviewed these Web sites to ensure that they are suitable for children. Many Web sites change frequently, however, and we cannot guarantee that a site's future contents will continue to meet our high standards of quality and educational value. Be advised that children should be closely supervised whenever they access the Internet.

Index

algae 7, 11, 27, 28, 29, 34, 39

amoebas 6, 28

anemones 39

animalcules 8

animals 14, 15, 17, 20, 24, 25, 28, 30, 31, 32, 33, 36, 39, 41, 43

antibiotics 10, 14, 42, 43

archaeans 18, 20, 21, 22, 23, 24

bacteria 4, 6, 8, 9, 10, 11, 12, 13, 14, 15, 16, 17, 19, 20, 24, 29, 41, 42, 43

bacteriology 43

binary fission 12, 29

biologists 6, 18, 19, 20, 42

budding 29, 35, 38

capsules 10

cells 4, 5, 6, 7, 8, 9, 10, 12, 25, 26, 28, 29, 30, 35, 36, 38, 39

cholera 41

cilia 10, 26, 29

Cnidarians 39, 40, 41

conjugation 13, 14, 29

corals 39, 40

cubozoans 39

cytoplasm 10, 12, 24, 26

decomposers 32, 33

diatoms 29

dinoflagellates 26

DNA 12, 13, 14

earthworms 43

Euglena 24, 25, 28, 29

eukaryotes 6, 24

fermentation 16, 35

filaments 10, 31, 32, 35

flagella 9, 10, 12, 26

flatworms 41

Fleming, Alexander 42

foraminiferans 27, 29

fossils 4

fruiting bodies 33

fungi 20, 24, 30, 31, 32, 33, 34, 35

germs 8, 10

gills 33, 34, 35

hermaphrodites 41

Hooke, Robert 7, 8

hookworms 41

hornworts 36, 37, 38

hyphae 31, 32, 33, 35

jellyfishes 39, 40

lichen 34, 35

Lister, Joseph 8

Lister, Joseph Jackson 8

liverworts 36, 37, 38

medusae 40

membranes 10, 11, 26

microbiologists 20

microscopes 4, 5, 7, 8, 9, 18, 24, 26

mildew 30

molds 30, 42

mosses 36, 37, 38

mushrooms 6, 30, 32, 33, 34, 35

mutations 12, 14

mutualistic relationships 31, 34, 35

mycelia 32, 34, 35

nematocysts 40

Nematodes 41

nonvascular plants 36

nuclei 6, 9, 19, 20, 24

nutrients 14

osmosis 38

paramecia 26, 29

parasites 30, 31, 41

penicillin 42

photosynthesis 11, 12, 25, 28, 34, 35, 39

phytoplankton 6, 7

pili 13

pinworms 41

Planaria 41

plankton 7, 13, 27

plants 6, 7, 14, 15, 17, 20, 24, 25, 28, 30, 31, 32, 33, 35, 38, 43

plasma membranes 10, 11

plasmids 12, 13

Plasmodium 24

pneumonia 12, 16, 42

polyps 39, 40

prokaryotes 6, 7

protists 20, 24, 25, 26, 28, 34

pseudopods 26, 28

radiolarians 27

red tides 26

resistance 14

sclerotia 33

single-celled organisms 4, 5, 6, 7, 9, 18

slime molds 28, 30

Spirogyra 28, 29

sponges 6, 38

spores 13, 33, 34, 35

tests 26, 27

tuberculosis 16

van Leeuwenhoek, Anton 7, 8

viruses 16

Woese, Carl R. 20

yeasts 16, 30, 31, 35

zooplankton 6, 7

48